21 Glances Into My Soul

Rawrie Bullock

BookLeaf Publishing

India | USA | UK

Presentation by *BookLeaf Publishing*

Web: www.bookleafpub.com

E-mail: info@bookleafpub.com

First edition 2021

DEDICATION

To my "littles" that bring sunshine to even the darkest of my days. April, Ariyanna, Adalynn, Grayson, Brayden, Tate, Nora, Mya & Zachary. Know that your dreams can come true!

To Mom & Dad, for raising me & teaching me how amazing true love can be.

To my siblings - for supporting me & always being there.

I love you all, I appreciate you all, you are my lights.

PREFACE

In my life I have know great love, but also great loss. Most of the poetry I write is me trying to work through the loss of that love, the loss of those people. Honestly, it is also me trying to remember them & the love I felt for them.

Who?

I am no one special.

No scholar, no teacher
No Scientist, no president
No Mother, no Wife.

Yet people will weep when I die.
I will be mourned,
I will be remembered.
As long as those who knew me live on.

But eventually that memory will be gone
and it will be as if Rawrie never walked this
earth at all.

Forget

I don't remember his voice,
his laugh, his cry.
I don't remember how it feels
to look into his eyes.
I don't remember how he smelt,
or how good it felt
to be held in his arms.

I see a picture in my mind
but alive it no longer seems.
He only appears real to me
when he appears in my dreams.

Can a person really fade with time?
Will I forget I ever called him mine?

Already gone are the memories of the surface.
 How long until
  my hand forgets how he felt?
  my body forgets his warmth?
  my soul forgets its soul mate?
 and finally, my heart forgets his love?

My friend

Repair my heart, restore my soul.
Nothing will ever truly fill this hole.

At his name my heart would take flight,
now it burns, in this never ending plight.

Greatly grieving the loss of one so dear.

I now go forth without his touch,
His love I will miss so much.

What I would do for one more embrace,
just one more look at his smiling face.

To feel his arms around me again,
to feel that love of my great friend.

He rests now, surrounded by dirt.
& I wonder now, if it will ever not hurt.

His face will forever be on my mind,
 the memories we made easy to find.

I will never forget you, my friend.
Forever you will live in my heart.

Void

An all too familiar sadness creeps into my heart.
I know the tears will not stop once they start.

A loss so deep it left a void in my soul,
the grief continues to take its toll.

I wonder when time will start to heal this
wound,
left by the lives taken too soon...

I have know the Joy of Love
    I have known the pain of loss.
I have drowned in that pain,
    and forgotten how to let myself love.

Love

Love if frightening

It is not blind,
    it opens your eyes to things you have never
seen.
It is not safe,
    it is the scariest thing you will ever do.
It is not cruel,
    the people who manipulate your heart are.
It is not free,
    it costs you your mind, your body & your
soul.
It is not unconditional,
    people fall out of love all the time.

Yet, as complicated as it may be,
    True Love is worth the risks.

Love carries no stopwatch,
    The heart has no sense of time.

Yearn

Is it because it is gone forever
    that I yearn for his kiss?
Do I feel him now because he watches me?
    Or do I yearn so for his touch
        that my body fools my mind?

I do Yearn,
    To see those eyes that searched my soul
    To feel those hands that knew my body
    To receive the kiss that weakened my knees
    To hear that laugh that warmed my heart
        Even the cries that tore me apart.

I Yearn for him now, like never before.
    To hold what is now bones in the earth.
    I yearn for his flesh, which is no longer there.
    To peer into those eyes, that are now two
black holes.
    To hold onto a hand where blood no longer
flows.
    To receive a kiss from lips gone cold.
I would lay beside him, give up my life. Just to
be by him, to feel close to him again.

I Yearn, because I cannot have.

Memories

Memories come & memories go
Sometimes they trickle, sometimes they flow.

Some we display for all to see,
others exist only in our memory.

Some bring happiness, some bring joy
All though, with our emotions, toy.

A single picture can bring you back to any day.
& the memories roll, as if on auto-play.

What makes a day worth remembering?
Could it be the emotions that the memory
brings?
Or the people that exist in that memory,
do they create the memory - the way it should
be?

Cold

If I die tonight,
    I die knowing I was loved.
With thoughts of family
    and the smell of love filling my car.

My return trip from the family farm,
    where we celebrated my upcoming birthday,
Was met with icy wind and blistering snow.
    Roads not meant for driving.

I can sense the shadows along the road,
    beings waiting for any unfortunate soul
to hit the ice as the wind gusts again,
    and find themselves in the ultimate peril.

A few cars swerved,
    narrowly missing the ice cold grip
of the shadows that awaited.

Who knows how many souls this storm will take
tonight.

Raw

Tarts in the oven
   cookie dough on standby.
A day of gaming and cleaning,
   turns itself into spring baking and cleaning.

My body, like my mind
   cannot seem to stop moving.
The smell of tarts baking
   fills my heart to the point of aching.

Squeaks purrs at the sight of me,
   Darwin is underfoot, tries to trip me.
      Houdini is curled, asleep, so happy.

In this tiny house,
   on this 3rd day of January
My life goes on
   Something a bipolar manic depressive cannot
always claim.

Life

Life, such a simple word to depict such an intricate notion.

The hardest thing we will ever do - live.

The longest,
    The greatest,
        The worst,
            The scariest,
                The most painful,
                    The most rewarding,
                        The most confusing thing we
will ever do.

Life - it is everything.
    The good,
        the bad,
            everything.

Miracle Dream

The greatest dream
    and the worst nightmare
I have ever had.

We were happy - married with kids,
    doing the things families do.
We had a great day,
    then fell asleep next to each other.

A dream so real,
    when I awoke, I reached for you.
Only to have to come to the realization
    you were gone, not just from the bed,
but gone from my life - gone forever.

A family we will never have,
    new memories will never be formed.
I remain, holding on the the few memories we
got to create together.

Pain

That Pain
    That life altering Pain.

The kind that becomes a timekeeper
    Before the Pain; After the Pain.

It cuts you to your core
    takes decades or more to heal.

Becomes part of your decision making,
    Do I want to feel that Pain again?

But all the Love, the Happiness, the Memories
made
    before the Pain.
The reasons the Pain is so strong.
Those make it worth it,
    worth all the Pain.

I want to feel free to Love again; free from the
pasts Pain.
How do I open myself up to the possibility of
that Pain?

Time

No clock, no stopwatch,
        no sense of time.

You cannot tell your heart
    it is too early to love.
Your heart has no concept of time.

Your heart, however, knows the pain of love,
        knows this may not last, that it may hurt.

So why take your time?
When you know not how much you have.

Tell them how your heart feels,
    Take the time, let yourself Love.

Choice

There in her hand, sat life or death.
Each one she drew, could be her last breath.
One is harmless, fifty deadly
She sits, her gaze held steady.
They were supposed to end her strife,
now they just might end her life.

But reason makes its way into her mind,
she thinks of what will be left behind.
What in life would she miss?
Family? Love? Marriage? Happiness?

The thought of it gives her chills,
she sighs and sets down the pills.

End

Her perceptions skewed,
　　Her doubts renewed,
He made a mistake,
　　to big to take,
Her heart is torn,
　　Her patience worn,
Love put on hold,
　　as events unfold.
No more pretend,
　　this is the end.

Disasters

Stomach feels like a volcano
    ready to burst.
Head feels like a tornado
    spinning out of control.
Body shakes like an earthquake
    right to the core.
Fever burns like a fire
    deep within her skin.

What

What is a mind
    that cannot think?
What is a hand
    that cannot write?
What is a voice
    that cannot be heard?
What is a will
    when there is no way?
What is a heart
    that no longer loves?

Loss

I don't remember what he smelt like.
    I will never know how she smelled.
I am flooded with memories of him,
    I do not have a single one of her.
His smile still haunts my dreams,
    I will never get to see hers.
I miss the feel of his arms around me,
    I will never know how she felt in mine.

I carry them both with me,
    but I would much rather have them here.
To hold, to love, to share, to live.

Heal

The words come pouring out my mouth,
  making my chest feel lighter.
I organize my words
  as I declutter my brain.
Knowing someone shares my story,
  somehow lessens the pain.
I stare at the empty chair as I speak
  as it symbolizes my empty heart.
The wound,
  even thought many years have passed,
is still so fresh, so painful.

The grief spills out
  little by little.
The way water leaves
  an overboiled pot.

Yet for once
  I see hope.
In the midst of that never-ending void
  a chance to grieve.
Through that grief, I grow
  and maybe, eventually heal.

Love

When I look into your eyes
    I see forever.
When my hand meets yours
    two become one.
When I taste your kiss
    I taste heaven.
When I hear your voice
    my heart sings.
When I think of you
    I think of forever.

No words

Sometimes words
cannot express
how we feel.